I0191470

21 Nights 21 Poems

Love - Found, Lost, Remembered.

Ekrj Parekh

/ BookLeaf
Publishing
India | USA | UK

Made with ❤ on the BookLeaf Publishing Platform
www.bookleafpub.in
www.bookleafpub.com

Dedication

The One who made my H*eart* believe too early,
and taught me how something so warm
can still end in silence.
You were the reason my nights turned into poems,
and why every word still carries your name
even when I try not to write it.
These *21 poems* belong to you —
to the laughter, the distance,
and the quiet Goodbye that never really left.

Preface

21 Nights 21 Poems isn't just a collection of words —
it's a story told in heartbeats,
written by a 14-year-old who fell in love too soon
and learned what heartbreak feels like too fast.
Each poem is a night —
a memory of someone who once made the world
softer,
and a reminder that even fading love
can still be beautiful when it becomes poetry.

Acknowledgements

I want to thank everyone who helped me turn my
feelings into poetry.
who listened when words felt too heavy —
you made the silence easier to live with.
To my Yayu —
thank you for believing in me when I didn't believe in
myself.
For every gentle word, every late-night talk,
and for reminding me that even pain can become
something beautiful.
This book would never have been possible without your
love.
And to the readers —
thank you for holding these poems close.
Every time you turn a page,
you bring my 21 nights back to life, one heartbeat at a
time.

1. Love In The Silence

I still love you in the quiet moments
when your laughter is no longer mine to hear.
Even as distance turns your warmth into memory,
my heart refuses to forget the weight of you.
I carry the fragments of our time together
like fragile glass,
every smile, every touch, every word
etched into me forever,
even if forever wasn't ours.
Though we are apart,
I trace your shadow in every corner of my day,
listen for your voice in every quiet wind,
and love you still,
in the silence where no one else can see.

2. I Was Hers And She Was Mine

Destiny Didn't Gave Her- Though She Was Mine,
No One Wanted Us Together *YET SHE WAS MINE*
When She Was Asked To Choose Between Me And
others, She Chose Others
That Pain Went Through Every Vein And Artery, Ended
Up Staying In HEART
Till The Very End, I Didn't Knew If I was Hers
But *She- WAS-IS-WILL BE mine...*

3. Found- But Had Lost Already

Found A Soul Not Body,
Found A Heart That Had Love
And A Friend Who Was Wanted By Everybody,

Left Back ALL
Tried To Let Her Be My All
As I Went Close, Saw That I Was Being Counted In
Everybody
Reality Gave Me A Check,
I *FOUND HER- BUT HAD LOST ALREADY...*

4. Broken But Holding You

I loved you beyond the edges of pain,
beyond the nights that swallowed your presence whole.
Even as goodbye became our only truth,
my heart stayed with yours, quietly, endlessly.
I would have given you every sunrise I ever saw,
if it meant you'd stay through one more night.
But love, I've learned, doesn't always mean keeping —
sometimes, it means learning to let go gently.
I still see you in every place I thought I'd forget —
your smile on strangers,
your voice in old songs I can't skip.
And though the world keeps turning,
a part of me still stands where you left me.
You were my calm and my chaos,
the reason my poems found their pulse.
And even now, as time pulls us apart,
my heart still folds itself around your name —
softly, painfully, beautifully.

5. Between Your Breadth And Mine

I want to live in the spaces between *your* breaths,
trace the curves of your fears and your dreams.
Your happiness will be my heartbeat,
your sorrow a storm I will face alone.
I will remember every scar,
every hidden hurt, every quiet smile,
because loving you is not about holding lightly —
it is about carrying you so fully
that even the stars bow to your light.

6. Your Pain, My Prayer

If I could carry every tear you've ever cried,
I would hold them in my chest until they healed.
If the world ever hurts you,
I would break in pieces to shield your soul.
I love you in ways words cannot hold —
in the silence before sunrise,
in the trembling of my hands when you are near,
in every heartbeat that whispers your name
even when the night is too dark to speak.
And if one day your heart forgets mine,
I'll still send love through the wind, softly, unseen —
because real love never begs to stay,
it stays anyway,
quietly protecting you from afar.

7. The Kind of Love That Burns Slow

You were never a storm —
you were the calm before it.
Soft voice, gentle eyes,
a warmth that lingered even when you were gone.
I loved you like time didn't matter,
like the world would wait for us to finish falling.
Every second with you
was a lifetime folded into one breath.
Even now, when the sky feels colder,
I still trace constellations in your shape.
Because some loves don't fade —
they burn slow,
quietly, endlessly,
until the soul learns to live with the flame.

8. Eyes - True Judge

When *An Arrow Of Love* Shoots From A Heart,
Before Touching The Heart It Goes Through The EYES
When I Passed Through Hers It Was Kind Of *BALL*
Which Occurred As Hayley's Comet..

Stopping Her From Going In Me Was Like Stopping The
Sun To Burn, Soon Realized It Wasn't Her
It Was Just ***HER EYES***

9. Weight Of Care

I carry your dreams like fragile glass,
gentle in my hands, though heavy to hold.
Every heartbeat of yours becomes mine,
every sigh, every joy, every silent wish.
I don't need to say "I love you" aloud,
because my actions speak in quieter ways —
in every word, in every glance,
in every moment I choose to stay.

10. When you Stopped Saying My Name

It's strange how silence remembers *you*.
How every empty night still breathes your ghost.
I try to forget,
but even forgetting feels ***like loving you in disguise.***
You stopped saying my name,
and the world grew colder by a whisper.
I still reach for your voice in my dreams,
still wait for a message that will never come.
There's a version of us
somewhere in the past, still laughing, still whole —
but I'm here, learning to live
with the sound of your goodbye echoing
through every heartbeat that never learned to move on.

11. You Loved Me In The Past Tense

You loved me in moments —
in stolen glances, in quiet smiles,
in the warmth of hands that never learned to stay.
I still remember the way your eyes spoke
when words would have ruined everything.
Love was easy when it was unspoken,
but silence, love — silence is cruel.
Now your name feels like a song
I can't stop humming, even when it hurts.
You loved me in past tense,
but I still love you in forever.
And maybe that's the saddest part —
knowing that something so beautiful
can still end quietly,
without anyone hearing the sound of a heart breaking.

12. A-LOT

She Was Given The Slot, For Loving Me A Lot
The Thoughts Of HER Ghosted Me A Lot

Whenever She Wanted To Talk To Me ,She Texted And
Called Me A-Lot
I LOVED HER,I was Optimistic For Her, missed her
YET SHE HURTED ME A LOT

13. The Way You Left

You didn't leave with thunder or tears —
just silence, soft and final,
like a candle deciding it had burned enough.
I watched you fade,
not in anger,
but in slow disbelief —
as if love itself forgot how to stay.
Now your memory lives between my breaths,
a ghost that hums in my chest.
I still reach for you in the dark,
not to bring you back,
but to remember how it felt
when you were here.
Because sometimes,
the hardest part of love
is realizing it ends quietly —
while your heart is still speaking.

14. Broken Soul Of Unwanted Heart

Heart and Mind - Trembled and
Troubled, not blaming anyone
Just realised that it was
me only,
Just from the other side,
who said It was her-My
another self, No she wasn't,
in-fact she was the one
who sealed my brain not mind,
cardiac muscle not heart
with sacs full of Love, who said I was
an option not a priority.

15. In The Dark

In the dark, your eyes do shine,
A twisted love, forever mine.
Beneath the night, our hearts entwined
A love that aches, but is divine.
Through shadows deep, through pain
and fear
I'll love you always, drawing rear.
for in the dark, where hearts may
break,
It's you my love for whom I
ACHE!

16. If You Ever Think Of Me

If you ever think of me,
I hope it's gentle —
not like a wound reopening,
but like a soft ache that almost feels warm.
I still look for you in places we never went,
as if love could leave traces in the air.
I still talk to the moon sometimes,
pretending it listens the way you used to.
You taught me that love doesn't always stay,
but it always leaves something behind —
a scent, a song, a memory that hums
long after the heart grows quiet.
And if you ever think of me,
I hope you smile once,
before you remember
why we couldn't last.

17. Trace Of You

You still live in the small things —
in songs that play by accident,
in half-read messages,
in the way my heart still stumbles over your name.
I've tried to wash you out of my soul,
but love doesn't fade like ink,
it stains deeper with time.
Every night, I whisper your name into the dark,
hoping the stars will carry it somewhere near you.
And though you're gone,
I still wait for the echo —
for a sign, a feeling,
that somewhere,
you still think of me too.

18. You Still Exist Here

I still set a place for you in my thoughts,
like you might walk back in someday.
The world has moved on,
but my heart — it waits, quietly, faithfully.
Your name still softens the edges of my pain,
like a scar that refuses to ache,
but never forgets how it formed.
Sometimes I see your reflection in the rain,
the way it trembles, the way it falls —
and I wonder if somewhere,
you feel the same ache when it rains for you.
You no longer love me,
and yet, somehow,
you still exist here —
in every silence I try to fill,
and every poem I swore I wouldn't write again.

19. Crimson Vows

If loving you is ruin, then let me burn.
Let my soul collapse beneath your touch,
for I was never built for gentle things —
only for the fire that you carry in your eyes.
Your voice is the storm I crave,
your silence — the wound I kiss.
Every heartbeat screams your name,
like it was carved with a blade and a prayer.
I would bleed in your memory,
if it meant you'd think of me once more.
Call it obsession, call it love —
I call it the only way I know to exist.
Because even if the world forgets me,
my ashes will still whisper you,
my soul will still reach for your shadow,
and in every dark corner of eternity —
you'll be the sin I never want to repent for.

20. Addicted To You

I am addicted to the way you haunt me,
to the shadow of your smile that lingers too long.
Even your absence tastes like fire on my tongue,
and I crave it, willingly, painfully.
I've kissed the ghost of your name
until my lips remember what your hands never gave.
Every thought of you is a wound I treasure,
every memory a blade I hold close.
Love me, leave me, destroy me —
I will follow you through the darkest corridors of
myself.
Because some souls are born to collide,
and I would rather break in your arms
than breathe without you ever again.

21. Blood And Roses

I would let you drown me in your darkness,
drink every shadow you cast,
and beg for more,
because love like this is not gentle —
it is a blade, it is fire, it is endless.
Your touch is a poison I crave,
your voice a storm I cannot escape.
I have loved you in ways that bleed,
in ways the moon itself would fear to witness.
If falling for you is a curse,
then curse me again and again.
I would rather be shattered by your hands
than live untouched, unburned, unloved.
Because some love is never meant to be safe —
it is crimson and raw,
and I would die a thousand deaths
just to feel you alive inside me once more.

www.ingramcontent.com/pod-product-compliance
Lightning Source LLC
Chambersburg PA
CBHW051002030426
42339CB00007B/449